SKUNKS DO MORE THAN STINK!

D. M. SOUZA

THE MILLBROOK PRESS   BROOKFIELD, CONNECTICUT

The author wishes to thank Jerry W. Dragoo, PhD., Mephitologist and Research Assistant Professor at the University of New Mexico, for his scientific review of this manuscript.

Cover photograph courtesy of © E. R. Degginger/Photo Researchers, Inc.

Photographs courtesy of Bruce Coleman, Inc.: pp. 1 (© Erwin & Peggy Bauer), 5 (© J. and D. Bartlett), 11 (© D. Robert Franz), 14 (© Tom Brakefield), 15 (© E. R. Degginger), 16 (© Larry Allan), 19 (© Erwin & Peggy Bauer), 20 (© Erwin & Peggy Bauer), 25 (© E. R. Degginger), 29 (© Erwin & Peggy Bauer); Photo Researchers, Inc.: p. 4 (© Anthony Mercieca); Visuals Unlimited, Inc.: pp. 6 (© Tom J. Ulrich), 22 (© Gerald & Buff Corsi), 26 (© William J. Weber); Animals, Animals: p. 7 (left © Mark Stouffer; right © Zig Leszczynski); © Marty Cordano: pp. 9, 13, 17, 23, 27

Library of Congress Cataloging-in-Publication Data
Souza, D. M. (Dorothy M.)
Skunks do more than stink / by Dorothy Souza.
    p. cm.
Includes bibliographical references (p.)
Summary: Provides information about the physical characteristics and habits of the striped, spotted, and hog-nosed skunk.
ISBN 0-7613-2503-4 (lib. bdg.)
1.Skunks—Juvenile literature. [1. Skunks.] I. Title.
QL737.C25 S68 2002
599.76'8—dc21 2001032958

Published by The Millbrook Press, Inc.
2 Old New Milford Road
Brookfield, Connecticut 06804
www.millbrookpress.com

CONTENTS

Skunks are very shy and gentle animals.

An animal about the size of a fluffy cat waddles slowly through the woods. A fox sees it and moves out of the way. So, too, does a raccoon, a bobcat, and later a bear. What animal can make creatures retreat or freeze in fear? Why, none other than the shy and gentle skunk.

Although skunks have a powerful weapon, they do not use it unless threatened. They will do everything possible to avoid trouble.

A bear cub once spotted a skunk for the first time. Curious to know what it was, the cub shuffled closer. The skunk hissed and stamped its feet to scare the intruder away. But the cub sniffed the air and inched closer.

Again, the skunk stamped its feet, hissed, and raised its tail over its head. The cub jumped around and tried to poke the tiny creature with one paw. Turning its back, the skunk shot a

Skunks are able to defend themselves against much larger animals.

Some skunks may be all white and have pink eyes. They are known as albinos.

smelly liquid into the threatening creature's face. The cub squealed and rolled on the ground. From that day on the bear cub avoided these black-and-white bundles of fur.

Many wild animals wear coats with colors that help hide, or camouflage, them. But the coats of skunks are a warning. The shiny black fur with white stripes or spots tells other animals that they better stay away.

About thirteen different species, or kinds, of skunks live in North, Central, and South America. They make their homes in a variety of habitats. Some live in wooded or grassy areas, while others live in desert and rocky places. Some skunks even roam around cities and suburbs. The skunk most common in the United States and Canada is the striped skunk.

This skunk lives in the Moab Desert in Utah.

Skunks were once grouped with a family of animals called Mustelidae that included weasels, ferrets, mink, and wolverines. But scientists have found that they belong in a family of their own called Mephitidae. The word *Mephitis* means foul smelling. You may find sources that still list skunks as members of the Mustelidae family.

A wolverine

SECRET WEAPON

Every skunk's secret weapon lies in two small sacs the size of grapes. These sacs are on both sides of an opening under the tail. They are known as scent glands, and most meat-eating animals have them. However, no scent glands work like those of the skunk, or have an odor that is as stinky.

A skunk uses its scent glands when it wants to let others know that it is nearby, or that it is looking for a mate. Skunks do not spray every time other creatures come near. First they give warnings like those given to the bear cub. If these warnings fail, the skunks will spray to protect themselves.

When a skunk senses danger from a predator, or threatening animal, it bends its body into a U shape. Tiny nipples appear under its tail, the glands are squeezed, and a yellow liquid,

This skunk is ready to defend itself. It's able to aim its musk at the enemy by standing in a U shape with its head and tail facing in the same direction.

known as musk, shoots through the air. Each nipple can be aimed like the nozzle of a hose at the face of the enemy.

The liquid may strike up to 15 feet (4.6 meters) away and burn the skin of its victim. It often causes brief blindness if it lands in the eyes. Usually little or no musk gets on the skunk.

When a skunk is running from its enemy, and can't aim its weapon, it sprays a cloud of mist behind it. Most predators give up the chase rather than be drenched by smelly, burning liquid.

Although skunks are often feared, they are really shy, gentle, and sometimes even amusing. They have some interesting habits and do more for the environment than most people realize. Let's follow a few of them now to see how they spend their days and nights.

Skunks are lively animals that can be fun to observe and photograph.

THE NOSE KNOWS

A mist of cool rain hangs over the meadow. As night falls, a female skunk stirs in her underground hideout. She is a striped skunk. She has a white stripe on her forehead that splits into a V along her back and ends at her tail.

She did not dig the hideout where she has been resting. She moved in when an opossum left. The place has kept her warm, dry, and safe on many wintry days. She is now ready to forage, or search for food.

As the skunk waddles into the open she sniffs the ground and nibbles on mushrooms. When she reaches a log she uses her long, thick front claws to tear apart the wood and uncover a mouse. After eating it, she moves on, letting her nose lead her to more food in the area.

Like other skunks, striped skunks eat both plants and animals. Fallen apples, grapes,

A striped skunk digs through leaves, under rocks, and in logs during its search for food.

Sometimes skunks uncover a nest of quail eggs hidden in the tall grass, or turtle eggs under the sand. This skunk is eating the eggs from a duck's nest near a pond.

berries, and nuts help fatten skunks before winter. When these are gone, skunks return to a diet of leaves, mushrooms, earthworms, salamanders, and tiny voles and mice. These small animals would overrun the countryside if they were not eaten.

Striped skunks help farmers by eating crickets, grasshoppers, and other insects that destroy crops. Skunks also dig for grubs, the plump, white, developing bodies of beetles and moths.

Skunks often dig into bee and wasp nests. Sometimes they are stung on their tongues and even inside their stomachs.

If they are lucky enough to find one, skunks may also eat a snake.

Grubs hide in the soil and damage trees, flowers, and vegetables.

When the weather is warm, striped skunks spend their days above ground resting in tall grasses, under bushes, or in hollow logs. Some skunks that live in cities or suburbs often sleep under decks or woodpiles. A few even slip into basements or garages. If no cat, dog, or human discovers them, they may often return to these hideouts.

Skunks enjoy lounging in cool, tall grasses when it's warm outside.

THE SEARCH

One evening, after several stormy nights have kept him in his hideout, a three-year-old male striped skunk senses a change. He leaves his den and stops near a pile of rocks. He digs beneath one rock using his strong claw, then grabs a salamander and enjoys the first meal he has had in a while.

After eating, the skunk then moves across a meadow sniffing under bushes and at the openings to underground tunnels. Not only is he searching for more food, but also for a female skunk. Mating season has arrived.

The skunk wanders in and out of empty dens for miles. He meets a young male skunk doing the same thing. The two push against each other, shoulder to shoulder. They snarl, push hard again, and then move in a circle around each other. After a struggle, the younger skunk senses that he is no match for the older one and slips away.

In many parts of the United States skunks are called polecats.

Two male striped skunks are shoving each other with their backsides. This is a mild form of fighting.

The three-year-old skunk finally finds what he has been looking for. Like all female skunks, she is smaller than he is and not as strong. He grabs her by the back of the neck with his teeth and mates with her. Then he leaves and will not help raise his young when they are born in about two months.

The pregnant female now prepares her den for the baby skunks. She chews up tender grasses to line her nest. With her front claws, she rakes weed stems and other plants and brings them inside.

She gathers bundles of grasses under her body and rolls them to the entrance of the den in case it turns cold outside. She backs into the den, pulling the bundle with her teeth so that it covers the opening.

Each day she sleeps, and each night she leaves to search for food. She must satisfy her own hunger and eat enough to nourish the young inside her.

A LINE OF KITS

Early one morning, four baby skunks are born inside the den. The kits, as they are called, are blind, wrinkled, and toothless. Each weighs less than a walnut. Although they have little hair, their fuzz already shows signs of being black and white.

At first, the kits are helpless, sleep most of the time, or wriggle around in their nest. When they

A group of striped kits sleeps together in the shade.

As the kits get older, they begin to venture outside together.

are hungry they suck milk from their mother's teats, or nipples.

By the time they are three weeks old, the kits' eyes open, and they become very curious about what is around them. But they are still not ready to explore outside. If a kit wanders out of the den, its mother will grab it by its neck and pull it back.

Most of the time the kits enjoy playing with one another by stamping, biting, and scolding. Then they fall asleep exhausted. If their mother leaves to hunt for food, and an uninvited visitor arrives, The kits may spray musk from glands that are about the size of green peas.

The kits grow quickly and soon begin to try other foods. They stop nursing at about two months old. Each night their mother takes them on hunting trips.

An owl can silently swoop out of the sky and carry one of them away, so they must always be alert. They follow one another closely in a single line. Night after night they learn where and how to hunt, where to find safe resting places, and when to use their secret weapons.

Striped skunks may have three to six young. Spotted skunks may have four to seven kits, and hog-nosed skunks may have two to four.

The kits go hunting for food with their mother and always travel in a close line for safety.

PREPARING FOR WINTER

The mother skunk's tasks are finished by late summer. One by one the young wander off to hunt alone and find places where they can hide during the day. The skunks begin to eat more

Two sibling kits hide and rest in a safe log after a long night of hunting.

during their nightly hunts, and their bodies become well padded with fat. Soon food will be harder to find, and the animals will need all the fat they can store.

Where temperatures dip below freezing, the

skunks do not hibernate, or go into a deep sleep, as some animals do. However, they often take long naps in their underground dens. Several females and their young may move in together if the hideouts are large enough.

Woodchucks, opossums, rabbits, or other owners of the den stay in different areas. They are too busy sleeping to even notice the new-comers. Sometimes a male skunk will also move in, but most of the time, males stay in their own hideouts.

The animals may sleep for several weeks or months without going out into the freezing cold. But as soon as the weather gets warmer, they poke their noses outside to sniff for treats. By spring some of the skunks are very thin and are ready to eat all the food they can find.

THE SPOTTED ONE

A skunk the size of a kitten sniffs the ground. It has a white spot on its forehead, one on its tail, and one under each ear. Many wavy white lines are on its neck, back, and sides. This is a full-grown spotted skunk. No one in its family has markings that are quite the same.

The spotted skunk has a lot of spots and stripes all over its coat of fur.

Sometimes the spotted skunk will do a handstand to show the alarming stripes on its back. This sends a warning signal to its enemy to stay away.

Most skunks avoid going into water even though they swim well.

It moves slowly for a while and then squeezes under a nearby shed. Here it finds a nest with a large egg inside. The skunk cannot crack the treat open with its teeth, so it rolls it into the open. It moves it backward between its legs, then kicks it with one of its feet. The shell breaks and the skunk enjoys a feast.

Spotted skunks are the smallest of all skunks, but they are definitely not the slowest or weakest. They are the only ones that will climb trees. They do not hesitate, as other skunks do, to jump into a creek or pond.

A spotted skunk puts on quite a show when cornered. First, it raises its tail and tries to make itself look larger. Next, it will flip its body and back legs into the air and take several steps while doing a handstand. If the enemy does not leave, the skunk will fall on all fours and fire its musk. It is actually able to spray in the handstand position, but rarely does because its bushy tail gets in the way.

The hog-nosed skunk rests under rocks and in caves and burrows.

THE ROOTER

A plump black-and-white creature sleeps in the shade under a pile of rocks in the middle of the desert. Its entire back and tail are white, and its fur is short and stiff. Its nose is so long that it looks like the snout of a pig. It is known as the hog-nosed skunk and can be found in parts of Arizona, New Mexico, and Texas.

The hog-nosed skunk moves out from beneath the rocks and begins searching for food when the sun sets and the desert cools. Poking its long, hairless snout into the ground, and digging with its heavy claws, it searches for grubs, other insects, and spiders.

Sometimes it uncovers a toad that gives off a poison to protect itself. The skunk simply rolls the toad in soil until the poison rubs off and then eats it. This skunk is also called the rooter skunk because very often it roots, or digs in the ground, for food.

On some nights, the hog-nosed skunk uncovers a lizard and makes a meal of it. If it meets a snake, even a poisonous one, the skunk attacks. The smell of an approaching skunk will often make a snake slither in the opposite direction.

If you ever meet a striped, spotted, or hog-nosed skunk when it is out foraging, try watching it for a while. Do not move quickly or make any loud noises. Remember, a skunk is really a shy animal and does not want to harm you or cause any trouble. Stay quiet and give it a little space. See for yourself how it keeps nature in balance by eating the many insects and rodents that nibble on our food.

Just make sure you don't mistake a skunk for a cat!

GLOSSARY

camouflage— blending into one's surroundings.

forage— to search for food.

grubs—the plump, developing bodies of insects such as beetles.

habitat—the place that is natural for an animal to live.

hibernate—to spend the winter in a sleeplike state.

kit—the young of certain animals such as skunks.

musk—a smelly liquid that some animals produce.

predator—an animal that hunts other animals.

scent glands—organs containing liquids that certain animals use to make their presence known.

species—a group of closely related animals that are able to produce babies with others in the group.

teats—nipples on female animals that their young use to sip milk.

voles—mouselike animals that can build underground tunnels.

TO FIND OUT MORE

BOOKS

Fair, David. **The Fabulous Four Skunks.** Boston: Houghton Mifflin Co.,1996.

Hagedorn, Maria. **Skunks and Their Relatives.** San Diego,:Wildlife Education, Ltd., 1997.

Lee, Sandra. **Skunks.** Chanhassen, MN: The Child's World, 1998.

Lepthien, Emilie. **Skunks.** Danbury, CT: Children's Press, 1993.

VIDEOS

The Growing Up Wild Collection**: Frantic Antics.** Time-Life Video, WILD Video. Featured are baby skunks, meerkats, sloths, and other animals.

ONLINE SITES

Project Wildlife
http://www.projectwildlife.org/living-skunks.htm
This Web site contains biological information, tips for avoiding skunk trouble, and a remedy for being sprayed.

Scent-sational Skunks
http://www.skunks.org
The official Web site of the American Domestic Skunk Association, Inc., includes great photos and a variety of information.

Striped Skunk
http://www.fishbc.com/adventure/wilderness/animals/skunk.htm
This Web site includes information on the striped skunk and many other animals, as well as photos and facts about the tracks of their feet.

INDEX